Contents   Page

written by Pam Holden

1

Here are the bones of an enormous dinosaur.

Tyrannosaurus Rex

Its name is Tyrannosaurus Rex.
We call it T Rex.

T Rex looked like a giant lizard, but it walked on two legs.

Its feet had three big toes
with sharp claws.

T Rex grew very tall.
It was taller than a giraffe.

It grew big and heavy, too.
It was as big as six elephants.

T Rex was very fierce.
Its teeth were long
and sharp.

Its short arms had two fingers with sharp claws.

T Rex was very strong.
Its tail was long and pointed.

It had rough skin like an alligator's skin.

T Rex was bigger and fiercer than most other dinosaurs.

Its food was meat.
It hunted other animals.

T Rex laid eggs to hatch its babies.

They grew and grew into enormous dinosaurs.

T Rex was the king of all the dinosaurs.